THIRD EYE

Simple Techniques to Awaken Your Third Eye Chakra with Guided Meditation, Kundalini, and Hypnosis

PUBLISHED BY: Amy White

Copyright © 2018 All rights reserved.

No part of this publication may be copied, reproduced in any format, by any means, electronic or otherwise, without prior consent from the copyright owner and publisher of this book.

Table of Contents

Introduction 4
Chapter 1: The Meaning of the Third Eye.............. 7
Chapter 2: Meditation and You........................... 21
Chapter 3: The Truth Behind the Hypnosis Curtain 37
Chapter 4: Kundalini and the Seven Chakras...... 63
Chapter 5: How to Open Your Eye 98
Chapter 6: Living Your Life Enlightened........... 124
Conclusion 135
Thank you!... 138

Introduction

If you're looking to open your third eye, you've already begun your journey by purchasing this book. Within the pages of *Third Eye: Simple Techniques to Awaken Your Third Eye Chakra with Guided Meditation, Kundalini, and Hypnosis*, you will find exactly what the title promises. There is so much more to spiritualism than what we see every day in the media, and this book will help you navigate through these murky waters to find the truths of the matter.

So, why did you check this book out? Perhaps you've always wanted to open your third eye. Perhaps there has always been an energy inside you, waiting to awaken. Perhaps the only thing you know about third eyes is the existence of the Three-Eyed Raven in HBO's "Game of Thrones" and you think that that sounds vaguely interesting. But the truth and the history of the third eye is not mere fantasy. It has been practiced by cultures all across the world since the earliest dawn of civilization.

This book will teach you simple, easy, and effective methods to follow in their footsteps. First, you need to understand what it is that we're talking about. We'll give you broad-strokes definition of what it all means to help you take your first tentative dip in the water. A lesson on meditation will then be followed by a lesson on hypnosis. Once your understanding of those pivotal practices has been cemented, you will be introduced to the seven chakras by our helpful guide; you'll learn where each one is situated in the body and how to open them. The lessons will then culminate in the understanding of kundalini, the most important of the chakras. Once armed with the necessary knowledge, you can begin the process of opening your third eye. An account of how this will affect your life and change it for the better will follow. You may even find some of the benefits to be wilder than you imagined.

The world today can be a hard place to navigate—dark, clouded with uncertainty, brimming with negative energy. If you want to surpass it, to rise above it all, then look no further. Whether driven by a lifelong passion or a passing fancy, you will reach the end of this book a changed individual.

Chapter 1: The Meaning of the Third Eye

The existence of the *bindi* has been something of a controversy in the Western hemisphere in the last two decades. In the 1990s, it was adopted as a fashion statement, without any research done into its cultural significance. To Westerners, it looks like sticking on a pretty piece of body jewelry. In truth, it is a custom dating back to 1500 BCE; it originally represented the third eye, and it holds a great religious and mystic value.

Our relationship with spiritualism and the third eye faces a similar cosmetic problem. The adoption of the practice by the hippie movement of the 1960s has turned the concept of the third eye into a fantasy, and spiritualism is easily dismissed by those who don't do their research. Meditation is a pastime for women with too much free time on their hands, and hypnosis is a farce. In fact, there's a good chance that you almost passed this book over after simply reading the title.

But dismissing spiritualism based on incorrect representation and lack of knowledge is the same as sticking a dollar store rhinestone on your forehead and calling it a *bindi*. Cultures all over the world believe in the spirit and in another plane where this spiritual energy resides. Meditation and hypnosis have been practiced under various names across continents. And wherever humanity seeks enlightenment, they find it in the form of a third eye.

With all this said, before anything else, let's get into some basic definitions:

Third Eye
So what exactly is a third eye? Well, it *isn't* a literal third eyeball in your forehead. It's a much more mystical and metaphysical concept. Historically, it

is also referred to as the inner eye, giving you the much more plausible image of a metaphorical sight. In art, you can see the third eye represented by a figure actually having three eyes, but this should only be taken as an artistic expression. The third eye is not visible, and it is not an eye in the physical sense. It is a spiritual conduit that allows you to see the unseen.

Enlightenment

Many times in this book, you will hear the phrase "a higher state of consciousness." This phrase is mostly interchangeable with the word "enlightenment." What are the mysteries of the universe? What is the meaning of life? Those who have reached a higher consciousness understand the answers. Of course, those answers aren't something that anyone can put into words; otherwise, mankind wouldn't need a thousand self-help guides when they have a simple two-page explanation available. In order to understand yourself, you must look with your third eye.

To put it more simply, everyone has a third eye. However, most people's third eyes are closed. But just because you aren't using it, doesn't mean it isn't there. Your gut feeling? It doesn't actually come from your stomach. And your sixth sense can do more than predict a change in the weather.

Spiritual Energy

Now, what about spiritual energy? We'll get more into chakras later on, but here are the basics. Spiritual energy is akin to the electrical impulses sent out from your brain, but rather than being biological in nature, this energy comes from the heart. If left unattended, however, it can grow weaker. Like any other kind of energy, we need to have a lot of it to complete any given exercise.

Soul

The Egyptian way of describing your soul, your personality, was the *ba*. In art, Egyptians would depict *ba* as a human head on a bird's body.

Metaphorically, this can have the meaning that your spirit has wings. Your *ba* can be thought of as something akin to your astral body, the one that leaves you and travels about when you dream. It can help during meditations to visualize your *ba*. Doing this gives you a more concrete understanding of the journey your soul undergoes.

The Astral Plane

Think of your body as existing on two separate planes: the physical and the astral. Physical represents everything material, the things you can touch—skin, eyes, nerves, organs—those sorts of things. Everything that we normally interact with exists on this plane. The physical plane is our world as we see it. For many people, this is all they see. It takes having a third eye to be able to look at the astral plane.

There is a concept in Celtic mythology known as the Otherworld—a world that exists alongside our own, but one filled with magic. Legends say it's where the faeries and gods live. When we die, our souls pass into this world. There are places where the two worlds' boundaries run thin, invariably called liminal spaces or ley lines.

The Celts may not have understood what a third eye was, but they were certainly on the right track, believing there were things out there beyond our normal sight. So, think of the astral plane as something similar to this Otherworld. It exists parallel to ours. In Greece, the term was used interchangeably with the etheric plane. *Aether*, referring to the fifth element, was how the Greeks understood spiritual energy. But don't go thinking of the astral plane as being some sort of mirrored reflection of our world. The astral plane is vast and limitless, unconfined by rules.

Are you starting to get a better understanding of the world we're talking about? By now you've heard talk about opening your third eye. You've learned about the soul, your spiritual energy, the astral plane. But how exactly do we go about accomplishing any of this? And why bother?

There are a number of reasons, and we will get into the more spiritual ones later on. Meanwhile, on a practical and fundamental level, what are some of the reasons why you should open your third eye?

1. **Intuition**

    Opening your third eye can give you intuition. Do you wish that your gut feeling were always correct? Do you wish you *had* gut feelings in the first place? Have you have ever felt something inside you, strongly telling you to listen, but you didn't? And later, after knowing you've made the wrong choice, did you wish you *had* listened? Having your third eye open means you don't have to think twice about trusting that instinct. It means your spirit always knows which choice is the right one to make.

2. **Stress**

Do stress and anxiety bog you down and make it difficult for you to get through your daily life? Does it affect your working or personal relationships? Having an open third eye reduces, even eliminates, those feelings from your mind. It is easy enough to say "everything happens for a reason" when disaster strikes, but a truly enlightened person understands the meaning behind those words. If you find yourself overwhelmed by the problems life throws at you, opening your third eye will help lighten that burden. If you find your anxiety medication isn't working the way you want, meditation will calm you.

3. Clarity

If your future seems unclear, opening your third eye will help you find the proper path to take. Many look to spiritualism as a way to cope with trauma, and many as a guide to finding life's answers. While the meaning of life is tricky and cannot be put into words, every individual has their own unique reason for existing. Opening your third eye will show you your reason and what future course you should take in order to benefit yourself and the world around you.

4. Empathy

Do you find it difficult to connect to the people around you? It can be easy to find yourself distanced from those you care about in this digital age. Empathy is something that goes beyond base emotions. When you have an opened third eye, you can better sense the feelings of the people around you and understand them in a way that words can't explain. This can be helpful not only in strengthening your relationships but also in healing the rifts that have formed.

5. Drive to Create

Having a blocked creative output is almost always the result of a blocked third eye chakra. By achieving an awakened state, you will open that flow again and be able to access your creative energy. Whether its art, writing, leisure activity, or something you do for a living, having your creative energy blocked is harmful. If you feel that you've never been a creative person to begin with, opening your third eye will awaken an entirely new side to you, and you will find yourself accomplishing things you never thought yourself capable of before.

Once you have decided that opening your third eye is something you need to do, the first step to achieving your goal is always meditation. What this does is to prepare your mind and soul for everything that comes after. It's like the warm-up before running a marathon. Meditation is an important part of every process; thus, you need to be adept at it before moving on to the next step. Only after you have become comfortable with meditating can you move on to opening your chakras. That is a long, careful process where we draw out energy known as kundalini. Finally, once you've accomplished that, you can work at last on opening your third eye.

Will it take a very long time? It's possible. Some monks spend their whole lives connecting to the spiritual realm, trying to reach the highest state of consciousness that they possibly can. But it's doubtful that we are ever going to reach quite the same heights as monks, so it certainly won't take a lifetime. In truth, the concept of time shouldn't scare you. When your third eye is open, you won't just stop cold turkey. Hence, rather than getting hung up on the question of "how long it will take," keep your focus on the small changes you feel inside yourself every day. Progress is progress.

So, are you ready to open a new chapter in your life? Are you excited to set yourself on a new path? Do you believe it's all crazy but want to see what we are talking about anyway? Are you Alice, teetering on the edge of the rabbit hole, curiosity ready to tip you right over?

Take that step. The first one is always the easiest.

Chapter 2: Meditation and You

For almost everyone, when the word "meditation" is spoken, three images come to mind: crossed legs, thumbs touching forefingers, and *om* being chanted in a deep voice. As cartoonish and oversimplified as it may be, these images aren't that far from the truth. Cross your legs as you read and see if that doesn't make the energy flow a little easier.

Meditation is the primary practice when it comes to spiritualism because everything that follows requires you to be able to meditate. The process is used to clear your mind of excess baggage. Think about how good you feel every time you clean the house, how you feel not only satisfied with yourself but also as if the world just got a little easier to handle. Meditating is just like that, except you are cleaning the inside of your head. This allows you to access spiritual energy without the worry of it getting caught on any snags.

Understanding is the first step to studying anything, so before you get started on your meditation, learn more about how it originated and just how widespread it really is.

A World of History

Though it has not always existed under the name "meditation," the practice of relaxing the body and opening the mind to spiritual influences exists in almost every culture in the world. The fact that many diverse cultures claimed to reach enlightenment—all by doing the same thing—is akin to testing a hypothesis. It's simply unbelievable that so many disconnected peoples would "invent" the same thing. And yet, meditation appears to be the same in every place and circumstance, perhaps for one simple reason: it works.

India

Yoga is a relaxing pastime for some and a stressful exercise for others, but universally, at the end of every session, a practitioner would simply lie on the floor and think of nothing. Consistently, that is the favorite part of everyone's experience. And there's a reason for that.

India is home to some of the earliest known forms of meditation. Hinduism, Buddhism, and Jainism all place great focus on the practice. Known in Sanskrit as *dhyana*, this form of meditation focuses not on emptying the mind but on zeroing in on a single thing. Time, diaspora, and assimilation have changed the context and meaning of *dhyana*, but the end result remains the same.

Rome

It might surprise you to learn that the Ancient Romans were meditating, but it's true. In fact, we got our modern word "meditation" from old Latin roots: the verb *"meditari"* means "to think, to ponder." Granted, when the Romans used the word, they used it to describe losing yourself in deep thoughts, not connecting to the spiritual world.

The Romans also had a name for the embodiment of the soul, one that is still used by psychologists today. The psyche, as we now call it, represents the collection of your mind, your heart, and your soul. Understanding that these three are linked and all part of the same system is crucial to understanding yourself. And understanding yourself is, in turn, crucial to opening your third eye.

Native Americans
Although the term "shamanism" came from the regions of Tibet and Nepal,

today we most commonly associate it with Native Americans. And for once, this is not a case of the white man misunderstanding, because the basic principles of connecting with the spirit world apply to both cultures.

Shamanism is the practice of using spirits to send your soul to a higher state. This has, historically, been used to heal, to communicate, and even to divine the future. It takes years of training, and the principles that need to be learned are more numerous than a single book could ever cover. Luckily, there's a way to incorporate shamanic principles into meditation.

Commonly used by Native Americans is the vision quest. Now, a true vision quest is a part of Native culture and not to be misused, but read the following simple steps and see if they don't sound familiar:

- ❖ Fast for four days and nights while sitting in a secluded area, one with spiritual energy.
- ❖ Ask the spirits for a vision to guide you, to help you find your way.
- ❖ You may experience a trance-like state and dreams that require interpretation.

In the end, this takes us back to where we began. Fasting for any extended period of time is not recommended, but sitting alone in a quiet place? Opening your mind to a trance-like state? That's what meditation is all about. And now that you understand it a little better, let's give it a try.

Techniques

There are many kinds of practices that have arisen from a range of multicultural sects, and a dedicated researcher could find at least thirty methods. Today, we're going to learn the three most common, tried-and-true procedures. Some may take a little more effort to pull off than others, and some may come more easily. This is fine. There are different kinds of meditations, just as there are different kinds of psyches, and the trick is to find what fits. As long as you reach the same place in the end, the path you take doesn't matter.

Mind Clearing

It is almost a riddle to say, "Focus on nothing." Repeating in your own mind to think of *nothing, nothing, nothing* means that you are, in effect, focusing on something. And many find clearing one's mind to be too difficult. The most important thing to remember about clearing the mind is that it will not happen immediately. You cannot simply close your eyes and expect the noise to vanish. The human brain is not a blank slate. It has to be erased, slowly and carefully.

The steps are simple:

- ❖ Get a mat or a cushion. If you are uncomfortable, that's where all your thoughts will focus on.
- ❖ Cross your legs. If you can, lift your feet such that they rest on your thighs. This position

maximizes the flow of spiritual energy.

- ❖ Close your eyes. Place your hands on your lap, palm up, right over left.
- ❖ Focus on your breathing. In, out.
- ❖ Start tuning in to the spiritual world rather than the physical one. Let the floor fall away and replace it with the energy around you.
- ❖ Clear your mind completely of everything. There should be no thoughts, only feelings.
- ❖ All that comes next is time and patience.

Results won't be evident on your first try, nor on your second, and probably not on the next several ones. Opening your third eye is akin to stretching a muscle. Every day, you hold your stretch a little longer. Thus, every time you meditate, do it for just a bit longer. Ten minutes at a time is perfectly fine. You can even set alarms for yourself in the beginning to minimize unnecessary musings of how much time has passed. Then, when you've managed to successfully clear your mind, do it for fifteen minutes next. Then twenty. Then half an hour. When you no longer care about how much time passes, turn off the alarm. Meditate for however long feels right.

Focused Attention

If you can't clear your mind of everything, fill it instead with only *one* thing. A mantra is a word or phrase that the person meditating repeats over and over. Whether you do this aloud or in your head is up to you, just do whichever makes you more comfortable.

The steps for this are also easy to follow:

- ❖ Use a mat or a cushion. Again, comfort is key.
- ❖ Sit cross-legged; place your feet up on your thighs if you can.
- ❖ Pick your mantra. Keep in mind that if you change it after several sessions, you can lose your progress, so be sure that it is the right mantra from the start.
- ❖ Close your eyes and hold your hands palm up on your knees.
- ❖ Repeat your mantra.
- ❖ You can set a timer for your sessions in the beginning. But for focused meditation, you can also

repeat your mantra a certain number of times.

While it is easy to get lost in the act of counting, you may find it comforting when you first get started. Much like the alarm, the purpose of counting is only to help ease you into daily sessions. Once you have established a rhythm, you can stop counting and continue to meditate for however long feels right.

Guided

If you've ever listened to an audiobook and found yourself completely zoned out, you've unknowingly practiced guided meditation. The world progresses and a spiritualist must also progress with it. Today's cold and technological atmosphere has distanced humanity from the natural spirits of the world, but we can find new ways to reach them through this very same cold technology that had pushed them away.

Guided meditation involves an audio source to, as the name implies, guide you. You can use anything from a meditation narration to an audiobook, or even a podcast. Much like your mantra, the importance is not in the words themselves. What you want is to let the noise block out your excess thought. Eventually, that too will fade.

The steps for guided meditation are similar to the others:

- ❖ Sit on a mat or a cushion.
- ❖ Prepare your chosen audio source. What you choose is up to you. Link it up to a device that can be

listened to with headphones. Press play.

❖ Close your eyes. Cross your legs and place your hands on your knees, palms up.

❖ You may hear the audio fade away as you meditate, but you may also hear it grow louder. As you feel yourself floating in a kind of void, let the sound become the only thing that matters.

You won't need an alarm with guided meditation as you can choose the length of the audio. If you feel that words are just too distracting, try ambient noise, lo-fi beats, or ASMR. After you've become adept at meditation, you may feel the audio is no longer necessary and can try one of the other kinds. But there's nothing wrong with continuing to use a guide.

Remember, vision quests called to spirits for guidance. And a main proponent of shamanism is the presence of a spirit guide. Shamans would go into a trance. In this state, you have successfully reached another state of consciousness. In fact, it's almost a little like hypnosis.

Chapter 3: The Truth Behind the Hypnosis Curtain

Nothing will make a person tune out faster than mentioning hypnosis. For many, it's considered a sham practice that has no basis in science. And with the overabundance of misrepresenting hypnotherapy in every procedural crime drama on television, it's not hard to see why. The long-held tradition of hypnosis has become poorly filtered through a modern lens due to lack of research and proper representation.

So, first off, let's peel back the layers and take a better look at what hypnosis is. The key to understanding hypnosis is to look at it properly. Understanding is key because hypnosis is very much a psychosomatic practice. It won't work if you believe it won't.

Now, saying hypnosis is psychosomatic is perhaps not the best move. "Psychosomatic" refers to something created by mental stressors, and it indicates that what is perceived doesn't exist outside your own head, which is not the truth in the case of hypnosis. It is not a placebo, and you are not making it true by believing it is true.

But hypnosis is built on the ability to open your mind, and if your mind is closed off, then it can't be penetrated. It's as if you've built barriers around it. If a hypnotist tries to entrance you and all you can do in response is sit back and think, *"This won't work,"* then of course it isn't going to work. So relax your mind and just open yourself to the possibility.

Before the Name

Back before we even knew it as hypnosis, people were putting themselves into induced trances. One of the basics of shamanism is the ability to put yourself in this trance-like state. It's important to note that, while in a trance, shamans could travel the astral plane. But mostly, hypnotism was used for healing purposes rather than religious ones. Spirit healing is a complex and convoluted practice, something we will talk about later on, but understand that when hypnosis first began, it had a strictly functional purpose.

Mesmerism

Frank Mesmer was a German doctor from 1780 whose surname we have to thank for giving us the term "mesmerizing." Though he never used the term spiritual energy in his writings—perhaps because he wanted to maintain a level of credence among his scientific peers—he did believe that every living thing possessed a vital life force. Much like the Greeks talking about ether as the fifth element, Mesmer was on the right track. But as time passed, the spiritualist community began to realize that Mesmer was not the first person to think of this vital life force energy and that naming it after him was perhaps giving too much credit where credit was not due.

The word hypnosis comes from Greek roots. Hypnos was the god of sleep, but he was not a god in the same sense that

Zeus and Poseidon are gods. He was more of a concept: he embodied sleep. "-*osis*" was a common Greek suffix meaning a process. Put together, hypnosis literally means "the process of putting one to sleep."

Showman's Hypnosis

Nothing quite makes one wince like the early 1900s slang "oriental hypnosis." What a perfect way to describe the way hypnosis was turned into a party trick by con artists in slick suits. Back in the day, the Far East was a place of magic and mysticism that people loved to pretend they could understand, despite doing no research into the truth of it. Anyone who wanted a career on the stage could find fame easily as a medium, or as a hypnotist.

This showman's hypnosis is the main reason we have such a bad misconception of hypnotism in general today. Hypnosis is not meant to instruct a room full of observers to climb on their chairs and do the chicken dance so their peers can laugh at them. In fact, it would be fair enough for you to not believe in hypnotism the way it is known today. After all, it has become garbled and disconnected entirely from the third eye. So instead, look at the history of induced trances and how they relate to our spiritual energy.

Hypnotherapy

In more recent years, as humanity has taken a step into researching the history and the truth behind induced trances, we have seen an upsurge in its proper use. One such example is the use of hypnotherapy by psychologists. Recall how induced trances were once primarily used as a means of healing.

Let's return to the idea of hypnosis being psychosomatic. Psychosomatic generally refers to anything stemming from the mind. Hypnotherapy stays in the mind, attempting to help treat personality disorders or other afflictions that can be hard to diagnose. It is still easy to dismiss hypnotherapy, but physical wounds and mental wounds manifest very differently. A physical wound can be identified immediately; it can be cured. Bullets can be removed and cuts can be stitched up. Physical trauma is even recorded at hospitals by marking X's on a drawing of the human body. Making these physical afflictions easy to understand is what we have doctors and surgeons for.

But mental trauma is not so easy to define. Despite the ever-growing and changing list of personality disorders and the constant academic research done by psychologists, we can never be too sure why things in the mind happen the way they do. While some view hypnotherapy as a last resort when medication fails, to others it is the natural course of action.

Techniques

Now that we have a better understanding of what hypnosis is and what it was meant to be used for, let's get into some techniques. When practiced hand in hand with meditation, what you'll end up doing is naturally going to be self-hypnosis, wherein you'll put yourself into a trance-like state. Each of the easy-to-follow techniques is a tried-and-true method, recommended by doctors and spiritualists alike. There are multitudes of ways to self-hypnotize, and you can try any of them. Remember, hypnosis is not meant to be used to control other people, so performing it on yourself means that no one else can take advantage or do it improperly. It is merely a more advanced form of meditation, with a more extreme endgame.

What follows is a list of the most effective methods of self-hypnosis and a detailed description of how to accomplish them.

Relaxation

This is many people's personal favorite because it involves doing your favorite thing in the world—relaxing. The downside to this method is that it isn't very different from meditation. Well, perhaps that's not an actual downside, but if you were looking for something different, this won't be it.

This method can also be difficult for some people, especially if they are the kind of person who just cannot relax. Your brain is always moving, the gears are always spinning, and you've never learned to turn it off. If you suffer from this problem, you may fall flat during the process of meditation. If this is the case for you, start with this method. You need to be able to clear your mind in order to complete any of the procedures in the following chapters, so learn to do this first.

For the relaxation method, do the following:

- ❖ First, find an area that makes you comfortable. Anything works, from sitting on a comfy chair to lying on your bed. As long as you aren't in danger of falling asleep, it can be anywhere you like.
- ❖ Whether you choose to have music playing is up to you, because some people can relax better in silence. But if you do have a hard time

clearing your mind, then music is a good idea. Thoughts can become louder in silence. It is better if the music has no words and does not come from a movie soundtrack that your brain could start associating with thoughts and images.

- ❖ Close your eyes; even out your breathing.
- ❖ Slow your heart rate. Do this by waiting for a moment in between each breath and making sure that each inhale is gentle and long. If you need to feel your pulse at first to make sure your heartbeat has slowed, that's fine, but do not spend too much time focused on it.
- ❖ Now, let yourself relax. Feel the tension drain out of you.

❖ By the time you have succeeded in this method, you will feel as though you are floating in a void.

There is more you can do with this method: a hot bath, scented candles, a massage. All of these can help you into a trance. The trick is not to fall asleep or forget what you were trying to do in the first place. Meditation with an extra dose of self-care—that's the relaxation technique.

Confusion

This technique is mostly used by hypnotherapists and not commonly practiced in self-hypnosis, but that doesn't mean you can't do it. Just try not to be too disappointed with yourself if it doesn't work, especially not right away. In this practice, the hypnotist attempts to confuse their patient into a trance. Thus, your goal is to confuse yourself.

For the confusion method, the following needs to be accomplished:

- ❖ Find an area that makes you comfortable. With this method, lying back is preferable.
- ❖ Close your eyes; even out your breathing.
- ❖ Count down from a large number, at least 50 or higher. Trying to sing "100 Bottles of Beer" in your head is a surprisingly effective method.
- ❖ Alternatively, count down, and on every second number, close your eyes. Close them on 99, open them on 98, close them on 97, and so on.

❖ You will have succeeded when the numbers have faded away.

The human mind has a hard time focusing on things like this for an extended period, so by the time you reach the 50s, you'll be drifting off into a trance. Some people won't even make it past 80. The downside to this method is that you may get too caught up in the act of counting. If you are unable to relax, or if you find yourself counting all the way down to 1 with no result, it's because you are too present in your own head. Work on your meditation first and make sure you are able to clear your mind successfully before attempting this again. You could also simply try another technique. Remember, not everything will work for everyone.

Visualization

This is the method you see used the most in crime dramas because it usually involves a patient remembering the night of a crime in perfect detail. This misrepresentation is what turns many off to the idea of visualization hypnosis. Being hypnotized does not mean you will suddenly have an eidetic memory. You aren't meant to remember things out of the blue or see things that you couldn't possibly have seen. The goal of visualization hypnosis is to lose yourself in your mind.

For the visualization method, follow these steps:

❖ Find somewhere comfortable to sit. For this method, sitting on a simple surface is preferable. Lying is not recommended.

- ❖ Close your eyes; even out your breathing.
- ❖ Start with something small—say, the sofa in your living room. What is its exact color? The texture of its fabric? Are there any stray threads? Can you pull them out, or are they sewn in too tightly? How does the light in the room affect the sofa? Is there natural sunlight coming through the window, or is it dark and overcast? Is it night? Are there lights on in the room? Do the throw pillows cast a shadow? Are there even any throw pillows on the sofa?
- ❖ As your visualization becomes clearer, you can now touch it inside your mind. Run your hands

all over it. Pick it up and feel the weight of it in your palms.

❖ Once you've truly managed to create this object in your mind, move on to the next thing. Say, the coffee table. Or the end table housing the lamp. Again, completely visualize it, down to the very last detail.

❖ You will know this has succeeded because you have genuinely entered this space your mind has created. In the same way everything in dreams feels real, so too will everything in your visualization.

The downside to this technique is that it is less about reaching a state of trance and is more about building your mental capacity. It is recommended that, if you use this technique, you also use another. Perhaps you can practice visualization for one day and practice relaxation on the next one.

Fixation

This is where the image of the swinging pocket watch was born. You may also recognize black and white swirls or a kaleidoscope. Despite their misuse on the stage, all these images do have a basis in real hypnosis.

Have you ever stared at a thing for so long that your vision fell away, and when you blinked back to attention, you cannot remember what you were thinking about? Well, you've unknowingly conducted a form of hypnosis on yourself. This is surprisingly the easiest method, and the most accessible, since all you need is an object to focus on. It doesn't even necessarily have to be a moving object; it just has to be something you can stare at for an extended period.

For the fixation method, do the following:

- ❖ First, find an item to focus on. Screens and videos of swirls or kaleidoscopes aren't as useful in this regard because eventually, the video will come to an end. Even a pocket watch will stop swinging if no one is there to swing it for you. This is one reason this method is easily dismissed, but it is easier to do than you realize. Just pick a thing, anything, to stare at. A box. A pop bottle. A dark spot on the ceiling. A smudge on a window.

- Now that you have your item, find somewhere comfortable to sit. Make sure the object is within a clear visual range. If you can, set it in front of you. If you need to, sit in front of a wall, or lie to down to face the ceiling.
- Don't close your eyes for this method, but do even out your breathing.
- Stare at your chosen item. Blinking is fine, but you should reach a point where your blinking slows or even stops.
- Sometimes, when a trance is reached, your eyes will close automatically. But if this doesn't happen, you will know you have succeeded when the item has faded away, as has the rest of the world around it.

This method, when used alongside meditation, is particularly effective. However, the downside to it is the open eyes. Though sometimes your eyes do close upon reaching the trance, they don't always. If they are open, your trance will be very light and easy to be snapped out of.

Body *Scan*

This method is the closest aligned to the practice of Kundalini; thus, it is highly recommended that you give this particular one a try before moving on to the next step. It is the one method that doesn't have any real downsides.

In this technique, you treat your brain as something of an MRI scanner. Many recommend starting with the top of your head and working your way down, but it is actually more effective to start at the bottom and work your way to the top. Wiggle your big toe, as the saying goes.

For the body scan method, follow these steps:

- ❖ Sit or lie down somewhere comfortable. For this method, reclining or lying is recommended. Stretch your body out as much as you can without feeling discomfort.
- ❖ Close your eyes; even out your breathing.
- ❖ Focus on your toes. Feel each one individually. Become aware of them. The skin, the bones inside, the muscles and the blood vessels in between.

- ❖ Once you have fully scanned your toes, move on to your feet. Do they tingle? Are any parts numb? Are your heels digging into fabric?
- ❖ As you become aware of every part of your body, move upwards and outwards. Take your time with each individual inch.
- ❖ Once you have reached the top of your head, you should be in a trance.

This technique isn't all that different from visualization, but because it puts emphasis on your body, it lends itself to kundalini more. But if you've been seeing the word "kundalini" several times now and simply have no idea what it means, worry not. We'll be swinging back to the body scan in the next chapter to explore it more fully.

So how do you know it when you have successfully put yourself in a trance? In truth, it varies from person to person, and it depends on how strong your spiritual energy is. A trance to you may simply be a state of mind where everything is calm, slow, and clear. You may reach a point where you have no thoughts at all, only feeling, and sometimes, you may lose feeling as well. The feeling of a mind untethered to a body, floating through space, is what many consider to be a successful trance. There is more that an adept practitioner with an opened third eye can achieve, but we'll save the juicy bits for later. For now, let's move on to the next step: opening your chakras.

Chapter 4: Kundalini and the Seven Chakras

There have been a lot of mentions regarding spiritual energy, but so far, we haven't had a clear and in-depth discussion on how to access it. What follows is a guided step-by-step course geared toward understanding and awakening your chakras and using kundalini. Opening your chakras is vital since your third eye cannot be opened if any of these chakras are blocked.

Chakras

Hindu practitioners of meditation have given us a very clear word to use for exactly what, where, and how to define spiritual energy: chakra, which is a

Sanskrit word meaning "wheel." Do you remember the astral plane? To recap, it is the second layer of existence that exists atop and parallel to our own; it is where all energy and etheric power comes from. You can think of our bodies as existing on two planes as well: physical and astral. Apart from our physical body, we also have an astral form. In this astral body, we are made up of certain kinds of energy. The energies that exist in this second plane of existence are known as chakras.

There are seven of these in total. If spiritual energy is a river that runs through you, the chakras are areas where the river pools and circles around. That is why they are compared to a wheel. Opening these chakra pools allows the river to flow smoother, which in turn leads you to a better physical, mental, and emotional state.

Opening your chakras does not necessarily have to be tied with opening your third eye. It can just be something you do to help yourself feel better like a spiritual juice cleanse. But if you are looking to awaken your third eye, simply opening the chakras isn't enough. As you do it, you must also engage in drawing out kundalini.

Kundalini

The practice of opening your chakras has long been tied to the mystic energy of kundalini. It stands for something that exists within our bodies, buried somewhere deep underneath physical barriers and mental limitations. Coiled like a snake, it lies in wait, ready for us to draw it out. Starting from the bottom and working our way up to the top, kundalini can travel upwards through our chakra pools and finally exit our bodies to the astral plane, connecting us to it.

Remember body scan hypnosis? That is the most effective way to prepare yourself for kundalini. By already become aware of your body and knowing how to work from the bottom up, you have laid the groundwork for drawing the kundalini out.

So let's begin to open our chakras. Each has a corresponding color, so if names are too difficult to remember at first, you can think of a particular chakra as a certain color. The colors follow a rainbow, rising up from the base of your spine to the top of your head.

Corresponding to each chakra is a meditative pose, so be sure your hands and legs are in the correct position before starting. If you have certain physical disabilities or limitations, do what you can to adapt and visualize the poses as closely as possible. Practicing visualization hypnosis which, as stated before, strengthens your mental power, makes this method more effective.

There are also crystals associated with each chakra, so having one near you during meditation is helpful, and you should acquire them if possible. Additionally, there are planetary associations, as well as mantras to chant for each chakra. Even if you do not normally chant during meditation or have a different mantra, opening your chakras is a different process from normal meditation. While it is not strictly necessary, it is highly recommended that you chant each mantra. You can also choose to chant silently, inside your head.

As for how you know when you've succeeded? Put simply, if you have to ask whether you have or not, you probably haven't. When your chakras open, you can feel it. The feeling is calming and cleansing, and it comes with the comfort of knowing.

1. *Muladhara*

The red chakra. Located at the very root of the spine, this is the chakra that represents foundation. Like the red clay in the earth beneath our feet, *Muladhara* is our base. It is most important to remember to open this chakra first as, without steady grounding, it is easy to fall.

Before actually sitting down to open this chakra, get yourself ready for it by doing some physical activity. Anything to connect you deeper to the earth is helpful, such as gardening or landscaping, or even taking a walk in nature. Feel your feet planted on the ground and do some stretches with both feet flat. Perhaps you could join a session of outdoor yoga.

Once you feel better connected with the earth, begin the process of unblocking *Muladhara*:

- ❖ Sit cross-legged.
- ❖ Close your eyes.
- ❖ Touch your index finger to your thumb while extending your other three fingers in the OK gesture and then place them on your knees. The circle made by your finger and thumb should be pointing upwards.
- ❖ Once in position, chant the mantra "LAM."
- ❖ As you meditate, feel the energy around you. Focus on the energy that feels red. Draw it in and

around your lower body. Take any energy that rises from the earth and add that to your pooled energy.

The gemstone connected with *Muladhara* is coral. This stone is the fossilized skeleton of red coral and ranges in color from orange to red to bright pink. If you have it in a ring, wear it on your ring finger. As coral was once a living thing, part of the earth and its ecosystem, you can again be reminded of grounding. The planet associated with *Muladhara* is Mars, the red planet. As the most visible of the planets, think of this chakra as being the closest to us.

The energy of kundalini lives just below this chakra. Once you have opened *Muladhara*, you can begin to draw your kundalini upwards. Then you can move on to opening the second chakra.

2. *Swadhishtana*

The orange chakra. The pool here is just below your stomach and deals with your empathy, sexuality, and relationships. There is a common misconception that in order to unblock this chakra, you have to give up relationships and attachments, but in actuality, it is the opposite. Opening this chakra means you will be healthier and more loving in your emotional connections.

Before opening this chakra, work on your personal relationships. Whether they are familial, with a romantic partner, or with a group of friends, or even all, it doesn't matter. Reach out to people and establish with them how important they are to you.

When you have strengthened relationships and feel more comfortable in all your human connections, begin the meditation process to open *Swadhishtana*:

- ❖ Sit and cross your legs.
- ❖ Close your eyes.
- ❖ Make a circle with your hands and rest it on your stomach, just below the navel. It should resemble circling the chakra pool itself.
- ❖ The mantra for *Swadhishtana* is "VAM." Repeat this, either aloud or in your head.
- ❖ As you meditate, feel the energy moving up your spine. Remember the tingling feeling in your lower stomach that occurs when you connect with the people you care most about—this is the orange

energy. Let it pool and swirl around in your navel until you have replicated that tingling feeling.

The gemstone associated with *Swadhishtana* is the amethyst. No, not every gemstone will match the color of the chakra. Amethysts are the purple variation of the mineral quartz, and it's historically seen as the most valuable. In Tibet, amethyst is sacred to Buddha, and prayer beads are made of amethyst. The color comes from the traces of iron in the mineral's crystal structure. Iron is one of the seven pure metals of antiquity and is known for being strong, so consider iron when you think of how strong and pure you want your relationships to be.

The planetary association of *Swadhishtana* is Mercury, the fastest of the planets. You can choose to interpret that in many ways, or not at all, depending on the context you apply it to certain relationships.

Once your *Swadhishtana* chakra is open, you will feel more comfortable and satisfied with certain human connections. Before moving on to the next chakra, it is a good idea to take some time to nurture these newfound connections. Your empathy should be open and strong, so use this gift to your advantage.

3. *Manipura*

The yellow chakra is located above your belly button, around the area of your solar plexus. Easy enough to remember: solar, sun, light, yellow. This is your fire, your will, your passion, and drive.

Before beginning the opening of this chakra, think of your own passions. What is it you love to do? What is your drive? Take some time to outline your goals, and be sure that you haven't lost sight of them somewhere along the way. If you feel like you haven't been following your own desires in the workplace or in your social life, take some time to outline a new five-year goal chart that will get you going in the direction you want.

When you have found your passion and feel ready to pursue it into the future, begin the process of opening *Manipura*:

- ❖ Sit cross-legged.
- ❖ Close your eyes.
- ❖ Place your hands in front of your solar plexus, folded as if in prayer, but cross your thumbs.
- ❖ The mantra for *Manipura* is "RAM." Chant this aloud or inside your head.
- ❖ Feel the yellow, fiery energy of your willpower. Pool it around your solar plexus.

The *Manipura* gemstone is emerald. The green variety of the mineral beryl, emerald has been highly sought-after throughout history as a precious gem. It turns green due to trace amounts of chromium in the crystal structure. Your individuality should be just as prized, and your dreams should never be tossed aside.

Likewise, the planetary association for *Manipura* is Jupiter. The biggest of all the planets, Jupiter can remind you that your inner fire is immense and should never be quenched.

You can feel when this chakra opens because your drive will be ready to shift into high gear. Before moving on to the next chakra, take some time to get used to your new willpower. Take the first few steps outlined in your goal chart. Set a new resolution for yourself and obey it for a week. This chakra is very easy to become re-blocked through laziness, so keep up your new passions for a while to make sure those energies remain flowing.

4. *Anahata*

The green chakra is located in your chest, right next to your heart. Compassion and unconditional love springs from this pool. As the midpoint of the chakras, it is the place for harmony and balance, and its importance is in keeping us centered.

Before opening this chakra, find your own personal balance. This may be in the workplace or in your home life, or it may be finding a balance of both. It may be literally balancing on one foot, as there are several yoga poses to help practice this. You may even harmonize with your favorite song on the radio. All of these things help us prepare to open *Anahata*.

When you have practiced balancing and feel at ease with yourself, begin the meditation to open Anahata:

- ❖ Sit and cross your legs.
- ❖ Close your eyes.
- ❖ Make the OK symbol with your hands by touching your index finger to your thumb, but this time, place your right hand over your chest, just above your heart. Make sure the three extended fingers are pointing upwards. Place your left hand on your knee.
- ❖ The mantra to chant for *Anahata* is "YAM." Repeat this out loud or inside your head.
- ❖ Feel the energy swirling around you. Remember, you should always be sensing the other chakras you've opened. Being able

to balance all of these sensations is crucial to *Anahata*. Feel the green energy pulsating with every beat of your heart: slow, steady, and balanced.

The gemstone assigned to *Anahata* is the ruby. A red-colored variant of the mineral corundum caused by chromium in the structure, rubies are known for their vibrant color and material worth. In many Asian cultures, rubies were laid during the foundations of a building for good luck. In the same way buildings are balanced, you must picture yourself solid and sturdy. Love is, after all, about balance.

The planetary association for *Anahata* is Venus, the morning and the evening star.

As Venus is balanced between dawn and dusk, so too should you be in harmony.

Once you have unblocked Anahata, you will feel balanced without and within. Keep up those balancing exercises, and notice how much easier they have become. As you are reaching the halfway point in opening our chakras, you should also be bringing your kundalini up every time. Picture it like a snake. Once coiled and trapped, it is now free to swim up the stream. As you go on and unblock each new chakra, your kundalini will swim up one level higher.

5. *Vishuddha*

The blue chakra. Located in the throat, this fittingly represents sound and communication. Expressing yourself is very important, even when it's not done through verbal sound.

Prepare yourself for opening this chakra by vocalizing. Talk, sing, chant, or hum. Make your vocal chords vibrate. On top of that, make sure you are communicating clearly in your everyday life. If you are unhappy with the way you have been treated, vocalize this. If you are happy, choose to vocalize that happiness—it will be returned back to you. Likewise, think of the inverse. Be sure to listen, and make sure people feel comfortable communicating with you.

When you feel that your voice is being heard, you are ready to open *Vishuddha*:

- ❖ Sit cross-legged.
- ❖ Close your eyes.
- ❖ Lace your fingers together, but inwardly, toward your palms. Touch your thumbs together. Hold your hands as close to your throat as you comfortably can.
- ❖ The mantra to chant is "HAM." Say this aloud or inside your head.
- ❖ Feel the energy of communication. It should be a lighter blue, like the sky. Let it pool inside your throat, alongside your vocal chords, strengthening your physical voice alongside your inner voice.

Vishuddha's gemstone association is the sapphire. Contrary to popular belief, the sapphire is not always blue. It is any other color variation of corundum that isn't red. The rare sapphire padparadscha, for example, is a salmon-like pink-orange. Keep in mind that sapphires, as close relatives of rubies, represent communication, which is essential to balance and harmony.

The planetary association of *Vishuddha* is Saturn, the planet which in Hindu mythology is associated with the sapphire.

Once your Vishuddha chakra is open, take some time to use your newfound skill in communication. You will find that the things you want are much easier to achieve.

6. *Ajna*

The indigo chakra. This is also known as the third eye chakra because it is located in your forehead, the place where your third eye opens. Though it is a common misconception that your third eye will open just by opening this chakra, it is easy to understand how such a connection could be made.

Preparing to open this chakra should consist mostly of self-reflection. Spend some time alone with your thoughts, and instead of trying to clear them, take time to organize them. Work on your intuition. Listen to your gut feelings, hone in on that sixth sense. If you are interested in astrology, take this time to really research your sun, moon, and rising sign. Meditate, in the Roman sense, on how they affect you or perhaps on how you don't fit your mold.

When you have done the proper amount of self-reflection and are truly ready, take a seat and begin the process of opening *Ajna*:

- ❖ Cross your legs.
- ❖ Close your eyes.
- ❖ Make the symbol for the third eye with your hands by touching your middle fingers together and extending them outward while touching your thumbs together and pointing them towards yourself. Fold your other fingers inwards. When completed, this should look vaguely like a triangle. This position for your hands can

strain the tendons, so it is a good idea to practice it and get used to the sensation before you begin opening this chakra.

- ❖ Chant the traditional mantra "OM." Do this out loud or inside your head.
- ❖ Focus on the way the energy here is smaller, condensed to a single point. Make that energy expand to become just as large as the other pools.

Ajna is associated with the diamond, the purest of gemstones. Diamonds are formed when carbon undergoes great heat and pressure, usually in the depths of a volcano. They are incredibly rare, precious, and valued. Think of yourself as a diamond, something to be treasured, undergoing great trials to come out on the other side stronger and more beautiful. Diamonds are pure, and it is the purity of knowledge and self-awareness that we seek.

Ajna's planetary association is the sun, bright-burning and life-giving. Allow the purity and heat of the sun to burn away any excess doubts and fears that are clogging your mind, and prepare to move on to your final chakra.

As your third eye chakra awakens, you will be able to feel any doubts and fears melting away. The remaining steps you need to take a clear in your mind's eye. Your kundalini, as it reaches *Ajna*, is now stronger than before and ready to connect with the astral plane beyond your body. As you move on to the final chakra, prepare to let that kundalini out.

7. *Sahasrara*

Finally, the violet chakra. Located at the very top of your head, this chakra connects you to the ether. It represents your enlightenment. Energy enters and leaves the astral plane through the top of your head, and if this chakra is too blocked, you will be blocked off completely. Likewise, if it is open, the rest of your chakras will flow smoothly. Once your kundalini has risen to this point and you have opened the chakra, the energy will flow out of you and connect you to the astral plane.

When you can feel that your kundalini has risen and all the other chakras are open and flowing, begin the process of opening *Sahasrara*:

- Sit down and cross your legs.
- Close your eyes.
- Fold your hands and lace your fingers, but extend your pinkies and touch them together.
- The mantra to chant is "NG." You will know if your chakras are not fully opened prior to this if the mantra is hard to say or pronounce in any way. Take that as a sign for you to go back and clean the other chakras.
- The energy of the astral plane is violet. You will likely not see this energy anywhere in the physical world, so be sure to draw it from the astral plane and into your body. Feel it as a great void.

The gemstone associated with *Sahasrara* is the pearl. Like coral, the pearl is the by-product of a living thing. Pearls are made inside mollusks by sand particles getting layered over and over again with nacre. Thinking of the pearl as being created by something alive should remind you of your place in the universe and how something so simple can become something so beautiful.

Sahasrara's planetary association is Pluto. Being the furthest away from us, this echoes how vast the universe is and all the knowledge within. Feel that vastness of violet energy.

Once your Sahasrara chakra is open, you will feel that connection to the astral plane. You will also feel your kundalini exiting your body through the crown of your head. Exiting doesn't mean leaving in this sense, for part of it still resides within you and part of it is in the spiritual realm. You must feel kundalini acting as a kind of bridge.

Now, it is crucial that you not expect any of these to work right away. Opening your chakras is not a single-step process. You have to start from square one and build yourself from the ground up. It could take weeks or even months, depending on how blocked certain chakras are. Each one is different, and thus, while one might open fairly quickly, others might be a more difficult process.

Chapter 5: How to Open Your Eye

Go ahead and give this chapter a read to see what lies ahead, but understand that you have to complete the previous steps before opening your third eye. It is recommended to first become adept at meditation, to the point where it becomes a part of your everyday life. Then you must open your chakras, a process that can take time, depending on how blocked you've become. If you try any of the following practices without completing the previous, they may not work. They might make you feel better on the whole, but they won't do anything about your spirituality.

Now, how to get started? Well, there is no "step one." Opening the third eye is not like checking off boxes—"do everything in this order and you too can be a three-eyed guru!" The techniques should all be practiced, every day, as a balanced new lifestyle change. Ease yourself into it, especially if these practices are unfamiliar to you. Let them become part of your life naturally over time.

Physical Practices

There are several things you can do with your physical presence to help open your third eye:

- ❖ Meditation and hypnosis, as practiced earlier.
- ❖ Practicing yoga, which is the most spiritually stimulating form of exercise.

- ❖ Using essential oils; these can help stimulate the area around your third eye.
- ❖ Control your breathing by counting and measuring the length of each breath. Do this during any daily activity.
- ❖ Periods of isolation. These are useful during meditation, but also outside of it.

Be sure that, during all this time, you do not let yourself become too isolated. If you cut yourself off completely from friends and family, it can be just as damaging as losing yourself in a job or retreating because of depression. Your mental wellbeing is key, and the upkeep of it is one of the many reasons people choose to open their third eye in the first place. Do not let this control your life.

You are in charge of your energy, not the other way around.

A Place in the Universe

If you have opened all your chakras, you should already have a decent understanding of your own place in this universe and how everything relates around you. Still, it will help you to think more about this.

- ❖ Go into deep, spiritual debates with yourself. Find a topic that you find controversial, maybe a social issue that isn't black and white, or a problem in the world that no one has found a solution for yet. An enlightened mind should be able to look at this objectively, and the debate should be calm and rational, perhaps something that could go on for days.

- ❖ Remember that for many of the issues you choose to mull over, there is no right or wrong answer. If they were easy problems to solve, someone would have done it already. However, don't mistake a complicated social issue for playing devil's advocate.

- ❖ A person with a truly opened third eye has no prejudice, and many of the constructs we've built in this physical world don't exist in the astral one. Perhaps you could take time to understand people with different sexualities than yourself, or someone unconfined by the gender binary. Things you hadn't understood before will look different with the third eye open.

Our old friends, the Romans, liked to consider meditations of this kind to be the greatest. It was a perfectly respectable pursuit to sit for hours and contemplate the world they lived in. We can do the same. As your third eye opens, so too will your perception of the world around you change and expand.

The Pineal Gland

The place where the third eye chakra resides, in your forehead, is pooled right around the pineal gland. This is a small gland in your brain that is responsible for producing melatonin and regulating our sleep patterns. Melatonin is the hormone that makes us awake or tired, and its chemical form is often used as medicine to help with sleep disorders.

The connection between the location of our third eye chakra and the power of sleep and dreams is clear to see. As we go on, we will talk more about the power of dreams and how they relate to your third eye, so keep the usage of the pineal gland in mind when we get there.

There is some evidence that harming your pineal gland can actually affect your third eye. The process is known as calcification, and it can occur if your diet is too rich in calcium or fluoride. Check the ingredients on everything you eat to try and regulate your intake of these two minerals. This is not to say that they aren't vital, because a well-balanced diet is important to your physical and mental health, and you certainly shouldn't forsake brushing your teeth. Just be careful that you aren't ingesting them too much. Drink lots of water and juice—they always help flush out your system.

Creativity

One of the benefits of opening your chakras and your third eye is an increase in creative output. This can be anything, whether you are a writer, an artist, or even a programmer. But these things go hand in hand. Participating in more creative activities will help open your third eye faster, which in turn will make it easier for you to create.

- ❖ If you like to draw, paint a canvas.
- ❖ If you are a sculptor, build an entire model city.
- ❖ If you are a writer, write a short story every day.

Aside from the examples given, engage in creative activities that you weren't too keen on previously, because now that you have access to the astral plane's energy, trying out new things will become easier for you.

A Balanced Diet

As previously mentioned, calcification of the pineal gland can occur if too much calcium and fluoride are in your diet.

- ❖ Cutting out dairy can be a start, even if you only cut it out on certain days of the week.
- ❖ Antioxidants can cleanse you, so eat foods such as blueberries and quinoa.
- ❖ At the risk of driving your friends crazy, take up coconut water.

❖ Vitamins and minerals are essential but sometimes hard to get to, so supplement yourself with vitamin gummies. They are fun, they taste good, and eating them makes you feel better every time.

Does a better diet go hand in hand with our earlier talk of psychosomatics? We'll *of course* feel better with a better diet, won't we? Well, absolutely. But if the diet is the only thing you change, "better" is the only result you'll attain. There'll be no connecting to the spiritual realm with diets alone.

Clothing

Eliminate synthetic fibers and go back to natural ones, such as linen, wool, and cotton.

- ❖ Keep your shirt flowy, almost robe-like, and your pants loose around the waist and ankles. If you can, wear a dress or another article without a waistline.
- ❖ Jewelry and ornamentation can also really help stimulate the flow of spiritual energy, but only if you use natural crystals and metals. The seven gemstones associated with the chakras are good choices. For metals, pure gold and silver, copper, tin, and bronze all work, but be wary of alloys. Rose gold, for example, is an alloy of gold and copper, but it could have been produced in a place with contaminants or it may have other unknown variables in the structure.

❖ Layering your clothing, again like robes, acts as an anchor and keeps all your energies close around you. However (especially when you're alone in your house), it can be just as effective to go in the nude!

Dreams

When you dream, your mind goes somewhere else. It goes to the astral plane. For those unawakened, it's a mere flitting visit—a passing through where nothing of value can be learned. But as you become more spiritually awakened, your dream-passing will become more of a solid, tangible connection.

As you become more awakened, remember your astral body. Think of it as having a more defined form and your travels having much more significance.

You may begin to experience lucid dreaming, meaning you will be well aware that you are dreaming as you experience it. In this state, similar to the trance, you are in an astral body. This process can be known as "dream walking."

- ❖ Keep a dream journal. This is one of the most important and highly recommended methods for opening your third eye. Remember, your third eye chakra is connected to the pineal gland. Sleep and dreams are more connected to spiritual energy than you realize.
- ❖ Take time to discern what your dreams mean, but don't rely on Internet guides to help interpret them. If your third eye is opening,

you should also be able to interpret them yourself.

❖ Once you find yourself lucid dreaming, try to make conscious decisions. Decide where in your dreams you want to go to and what you want to see happen. Every morning, record the journey you've taken the previous night.

Those we've just covered are all ways to open your third eye that involve everyday practices, things you can do easily that are tied into humanity. If you were looking to be enlightened to feel a sense of peace with yourself and less afraid of the future—to be cleaner and happier with life—those steps are all you need. Continue them even after you feel your third eye open; keep the practices up. It's easy enough for chakras to get clogged up again, and your third eye will close. Fortunately, they aren't hard to maintain, as all of these practices make you healthier even when unconnected to the spirit, raising your endorphins which in turn urges you to continue. Your third eye will stay open and you will feel content.

However, if you are curious about the power held by the shamans of the ancient world, want to explore all the facets of spirituality, and wish to see just how far you can go with an opened third eye, try some of the following techniques.

Scrying

If you think crystal balls are confined to fortune-tellers at school carnivals, think again. The practice of scrying goes back to Mesoamerican cultures and even to Ancient Persia. The best part of it is that you don't need crystals to try it.

Scrying is the act of reading visions and prophecies seen through any reflective surface. It is not only the future you can see but oftentimes the present or the past as well. There are three items most commonly used for scrying, and they have the greatest potential for success: crystals, water, and mirrors.

For crystals

- ❖ Use a ball or a rough, uncut crystal, as long as it has a bit of surface that is smooth and reflective.
- ❖ Quartz is traditionally used, but obsidian and jade are two stones with high spiritual significance. All three are easy to get your hands on, especially quartz and obsidian, which can be found at any gem store or tourist stop.
- ❖ Recall the seven gemstones that were used to open your chakras. If you have any of those on hand, and if any are large enough to see visions through, use them.

For water

- ❖ If you want to go the traditional route, fill a silver bowl. Of course, any old porcelain bowl could do the trick, but choosing a bowl of clay or something else earthen can strengthen spiritual ties.
- ❖ A local lake or a reflective pond can also be used, but in those cases, you should watch out for pedestrians or other interruptions.

For mirrors

- ❖ You can use any kind—a floor-length wall mirror, a handheld mirror, even the compact you carry around in your purse.

- ❖ If you want maximum effect, browse around gemstone or Wicca shops for a black mirror. Made from obsidian, these were the kind of mirrors used by Mesoamerican cultures. They believed these mirrors were the portal to another world, and they weren't wrong. Black mirrors open a doorway to the astral plane, and your visions will be clearest and strongest through them.

Steps to perform the act of scrying

- ❖ Sit as you would in a meditative pose, but place the tool in front of you.
- ❖ Surround yourself with scented candles if you can. Background,

ambient music can also set the mood.

❖ Stare into the reflective surface and connect to the astral plane through it.

The practice is not all different from meditation, but it requires much more concentration and effort. You must truly feel the connection to your spiritual energy. If your third eye is not all the way open, you won't be successful, but that doesn't mean you should stop trying. Think of it as schooling. You never master a subject on your first day.

Automatic Writing

Don't confuse this with the act of free writing. Even though free writing is a worthy pursuit for those who like to write, it is completely unconnected to the mystic arts. Automatic writing invites the astral energy to come through our bodies and out through our hands. It has often been misused by mediums who claim that ghosts take control of their hands. In truth, true automatic writing won't produce anything really legible. Much in the same way dreams stop making sense once you wake up, the words written during automatic writing will cease to make sense once you leave the trance.

In order to perform automatic writing, do the following:

- ❖ Put yourself in an induced trance using one of the self-hypnosis techniques taught earlier.
- ❖ Instead of lying completely still, keep a pen or pencil in hand and a piece of paper in front.

- ❖ As you begin the process of self-hypnosis, move your hand around. You don't have to form proper words or letters; the important part is the movement. As you enter the trance, your moving hand will draw from the energies of the astral plane and begin to write on its own.

Practice this even if the words you write make no sense. Practice this even if you don't write words at all. The very act of tapping the astral plane opens the eye, and the more you do it, the more you might find you've written something of value. Don't be afraid if you start writing in other languages or even other alphabets, either. That's perfectly normal, even something to be pursued.

Levitation

The hardest out there and the most common when we think of spirituality. But even if you go your whole life without managing to lift an inch off the floor, the pursuit of levitation energizes and exercises your third eye.

- ❖ In Hinduism, some believe levitation can be done once you have mastered yoga. Perhaps after a yoga session, you can meditate and attempt to lift off the ground.
- ❖ Mostly, the art of levitation is achieved by picturing the act of floating. During a session of visualization hypnosis, see yourself rising in the air.
- ❖ You can also play with the feeling of levitation by tricking your arms into it. Stand in a doorway and

press the back of your hands against the frame. Continue applying pressure for as long as you can, then step out. Your arms will rise of their own accord. This is not actual levitation, of course, but pay attention to the feeling of rising and of weightlessness in your arms.

It takes time to open your third eye. Again, it is imperative that you don't attempt it before you are ready. Many of these practices, especially those that lean toward the paranormal, require you to be adept at meditation and hypnosis. Your chakras absolutely need to be open, and your kundalini must be flowing. If you attempt to open your third eye before you're prepared, at best, nothing will happen and this text will seem like a fraud. At worst, you could find yourself subjected to nightmares and sleep paralysis, and your top two chakras—*Ajna* and *Sahasrara*—could get blocked completely and irrevocably.

Scared yet? Don't be. You've already read all the practices, and you know what you're doing. You know where to start, and you know every step to take along the path. Take as much time as you feel you need. Don't be afraid to wait periods of time in between. Just because you've mastered meditation, doesn't mean you need to immediately put yourself in a trance. Just keep at the meditation every day. Remember, this book is only here to help and guide you along your way.

Chapter 6: Living Your Life Enlightened

Now, if you've made it all the way to this point and haven't attempted any of the techniques, it's most likely because you're wondering, what's the point? Why bother? Well, if understanding the meaning of life wasn't enough of a temptation, let's talk about the many benefits of opening your third eye.

In George Lucas' movie epic, the *Star Wars* saga, the Jedi Order tap into something called the Force. Science fantasy, maybe? Cultural appropriation, definitely. Although, perhaps due to the respect and reverence he gave to the idea that the monks were the most "good" and the most powerful beings in the universe, we can forgive Lucas this character flaw.

While writing *Star Wars* and creating the universe they lived in, Lucas did his research. The Force is not unlike the astral energy that we connect to when we open our third eye. But moving things telepathically and playing mind tricks? Surely, that's all make-believe. Or is it?

There are a whole host of benefits that can come from opening your third eye, ranging from the practical to the out-of-this-world. The most base of these reasons, however, is simply that being third-eye blind is miserable. You feel clogged, stuck in one place. Maybe you're ready for a midlife crisis and you aren't even halfway through your twenties yet. So, opening your third eye can give you that sense of belonging you've been seeking. It can free you from feeling trapped and make you a happier, healthier person all around.

But as the techniques to opening your third eye range from grounded to out-of-this-world, so too can the effects that come with it. Read on to discover some of the things you may find yourself accomplishing.

## *Second					Sight*

Sometimes, the third eye can be referred to as a sixth sense. Don't mistake that to mean you'll be able to see dead people. Although making connections with the souls who have passed on and reside in the astral plane is not uncommon, it is far from the only thing the second sight allows you to do. Remember how the astral plane exists alongside but separate to our own, invisible to the naked eye? Many people with an opened third eye report seeing this astral plane, overlaying our own world. Although unsettling at first, seeing our world at more than face value can be a comfort.

Second sight comes alongside scrying, as it looks beyond what we see with a normal pair of eyes. But the second sight is not confined to a reflective surface, because once our third eye is open, we can begin to see these visions inside our mind. Seeing the past, present, or future is common. Remote viewing—that is, witnessing events taking place somewhere far away and in a place you've never seen before—is also common.

Past Life Regression

Not every culture believes in past lives and not everyone that do believe it does so in quite the same way. The mysteries of the past life are reserved for those who've reached enlightenment, and even then, you might never truly understand how reincarnation works. It seems that it varies entirely on a person-to-person basis, because your soul might have lived a hundred lives before this one, and it might be newly existing—some souls may have lived once a thousand years ago and stayed in the spirit world immediately afterward.

But if you do happen to be a soul with a past life or two under your belt, having visions and reliving pieces of these lives is something you can find happening once you open your third eye.

Sometimes, it can be brought on by you by seeking it out during meditation or a trance. But sometimes, it can come to you unbidden during sleep.

Reliving a bit of your past life can be a wild and exciting experience. So many people dream of seeing the world as it was in the past, and for a brief moment, you too might be able to find yourself in it.

Auras

Although it can have no real benefits, seeing people's auras is a fun bonus that comes alongside enlightenment. A person's aura is the spiritual energy that surrounds them, sometimes manifesting as a halo. Colors indicate traits in someone's personality, and darker auras indicate a person whose energy is clogged. It is nice to be able to get a sense for someone before even speaking with them, and it will help you understand complicated people, healing relationships that have been muddied through lack of communication.

Following is a quick rundown on what the variety of aura colors may indicate in an individual:

- ❖ Red is passion. Darker red indicates someone controlled by their anger while a brighter red indicates love and power.
- ❖ Orange is courage and confidence.
- ❖ Yellow is intelligence and optimism.
- ❖ Green is a love of nature and the earth.

- ❖ Aquamarine is reserved for healers.
- ❖ Blue indicates calm and caring sensitivity.
- ❖ Indigo means someone has awakened their third eye, so you should always see a little indigo in your own aura.
- ❖ Purple is creativity and imagination.
- ❖ White is purity and truth.

Most people have more than one aura color, sometimes separate and sometimes mixing their dominant traits together. If you see an individual, especially someone you are close to, with a muddied grey or brown sheen to their aura, it means their chakras are blocked and they are losing touch with their own spiritual energy. This is always accompanied by personal problems, insecurities, grief, or hatred. Reach out to this person and try to help them any way you can, whether spiritually or just in their personal life. You can always recommend them this book.

Astral Projection

Finally, we return to the land of dreams. In our previous chapter, when discussing the use of a dream journal, we talked about dream walking. Astral projection is the highest stage that someone who has mastered control of their dreams can reach.

As you have been lucid dreaming, you have been able to dream walk. Now you must stop walking and really take a look around you. Remember, when we dream, our souls go to the astral plane. Once you have completely mastered yourself in this plane while in your astral form, you can travel anywhere you wish to go.

Astral projection can manifest anywhere in the physical world or the astral one. You can do anything from visiting a foreign nation to reaching the farthest recesses of the universe. Nothing is outside the possibilities. You can even visit other people's dreams.

And if you are truly interested in following the path of spiritualism, there is even more that can be accomplished once your third eye is open. Mastering it is difficult and takes years of concentration, but if you are already continuing these practices every day, it's not out of the realm of possibility to expect that you could grow to find new abilities. Communication with souls who have passed on. Telepathy. Telekinesis. You may even achieve levitation.

Of course, you might only be doing this because you want to wake up in the morning and actually feel awake. This is as perfectly noble a quest. Sometimes, you don't need the fancy bells and whistles to feel good and happy and at peace with yourself. You may not even want them if some of the awakenings seem too outlandish for you. Opening the third eye is about finding that inner balance in order to know exactly what you need to make yourself happy.

Conclusion

If you've read to the end, you won't need me to tell you that your third eye has begun to open. And perhaps the cynic in you will scoff, but the simple fact of the matter is, knowledge is the first step to any spiritual practice. Even if you haven't performed a single thing recommended, now you know how. Now it is there in your psyche.

But if you have started? Now you can feel it. You've meditated, you've opened your chakras, and you've become a conduit for the flow of the universe. Next? Repetition. Don't let yourself fall out of practice. Don't let this become something you do once, out of curiosity. Don't let this become something you do once every three months because you've got some spare time.

Set a schedule for yourself. Put aside some time every day to meditate. Put yourself in a trance every Sunday night. Work on opening those chakras, one by one. It may take months or it may take even longer, but remember the monks who put themselves in isolation for years to reach enlightenment. Remember that, as you keep at it, your energy will grow stronger. Notice the auras of the people around you. Keep a dream journal. Feel the change in yourself as you become calmer, more centered.

The world we live in today is scary. It's clouded by dark energy and filled with uncertainty. Natural disasters, a failing economy, and an unstable sociopolitical climate make it hard sometimes to even get out of bed in the morning. The younger generation doesn't see a future to look forward to. The Mayans predicted our world would end in 2012, and some days it seems possible that they were right all along.

But we are not without hope. Every negative has an opposing positive. Find your own comfort in this world, knowing that it isn't the only world out there. Take on this world with the enlightenment and all the powers of the astral plane, with three eyes open. Walk in your dreams. Breathe deeper. Live better.

In fact, just live.

Thank you!

Before you go, I just wanted to say thank you for purchasing my book.

You could have picked from dozens of other books on the same topic but you took a chance and chose this one.

So, a HUGE thanks to you for getting this book and for reading all the way to the end.

Now I wanted to ask you for a small favor. **Could you please take just a few minutes to leave a review for this book?**

This feedback will help me continue to write the type of books that will help you get the results you want. So if you enjoyed it, please let me know! (-:

www.ingramcontent.com/pod-product-compliance
Lightning Source LLC
Chambersburg PA
CBHW052059110526
44591CB00013B/2270